CONTEMPORARY LIVES

TAYLOR SWIFT

COUNTRY & POP SUPERSTAR

ABDO
Publishing Company

CONTEMPORARY LIVES

TAYLOR SWIFT

COUNTRY & POP SUPERSTAR

by Melissa Higgins

CREDITS

Published by ABDO Publishing Company, PO Box 398166, Minneapolis, MN 55439. Copyright © 2012 by Abdo Consulting Group, Inc. International copyrights reserved in all countries. No part of this book may be reproduced in any form without written permission from the publisher. The Essential Library™ is a trademark and logo of ABDO Publishing Company.

Printed in the United States of America,
North Mankato, Minnesota
112011
012012

 THIS BOOK CONTAINS AT LEAST 10% RECYCLED MATERIALS.

Editor: Lauren Coss
Copy Editor: Angela Wiechmann
Series design: Emily Love
Cover and interior production: Kelsey Oseid

Library of Congress Cataloging-in-Publication Data
Higgins, Melissa, 1953-
  Taylor Swift : country & pop superstar / by Melissa Higgins.
       p. cm. -- (Contemporary lives)
  Includes bibliographical references and index.
  ISBN 978-1-61783-327-4
  1. Swift, Taylor, 1989---Juvenile literature. 2. Women country musicians--United States--Biography--Juvenile literature. I. Title.
  ML3930.S989H54 2012
  782.421642092--dc23
  [B]
                                        2011042571

TABLE OF CONTENTS

Taylor Swift's Fearless Tour brought her songs to life for her fans around the world.

CHAPTER 1
Her Diary Brought to Life

||||||||||||||||||||||||||||||||||||||||||||||||||||||||||||||||||||||||||||||||||||||||

Dressed in high school band uniforms with giant plumed helmets, Taylor Swift and the members of her band stood backstage in a circle. They each stuck one foot in the middle of the circle, and one of them gave a speech. Then, as if they were about to march onto a high school football field, they shouted in unison, 'Let's go out there and be fearless!"[1]

While many people think 13 is an unlucky number, it's not for Swift. She was born on the thirteenth of December, turned 13 on Friday the thirteenth, her first album went gold in 13 weeks, and her first song has a 13-second intro. The number is painted on the door of her tour bus and on the head of the drummer's drum. According to Swift, she draws 13 on her hand before she goes onstage because she wants to have it with her for good luck.

Inside the auditorium, accompanied by her band's musical intro and the screaming audience, Swift rose on an elevator platform, her spangled white and gold helmet and uniform slowly coming into glittering view. Thousands of fans sang along as she began her hit song "You Belong With Me," with its lyrics about a girl in a high school band pining for a boy with a cheerleader girlfriend:

> But she wears short skirts
> I wear T-shirts
> She's cheer captain
> And I'm on the bleachers[2]

With her lucky number 13 drawn in large digits on the back of her hand, Swift marched and skipped up and down the stage. Lights flashed across the set, dancers performed cheerleading maneuvers. Toward the end of the song, two dancers ripped off Swift's band uniform, revealing a short and shiny silver dress covered with sparkling beads. She grabbed a guitar and played along with the band and at the song's finish, swinging her long blonde hair as she bowed to her cheering and adoring fans.

The entire effect—lighting, dancing, set, costumes—was dramatic and theatrical, just how Swift had always imagined diary songs would look brought to life. Here she was, headlining her own tour for the first time with thousands of fans cheering her on. But life had not always been so glamorous for Swift.

||||||||||||||||||||||||||||||||||||||||||||||||||||||

THE MEAN GIRLS

Growing up in Pennsylvania, Swift had been on the outside. Girls she thought were her friends wouldn't hang out with her. At school, the girls moved away from the lunch table when she sat down. They heckled her in the hallways about her country music singing.

Swift had known these girls for as long as she could remember, and she didn't understand why they were rejecting her. Tall and gawky with frizzy blonde hair, Swift didn't look like the cool girls. And in the town where she lived, country music was definitely uncool.

Swift could have lost herself in bitterness over her life's frustrating and confusing turns, but instead she learned to accept herself. At the age of 12, she began releasing her emotions into song lyrics, writing music as if she were writing a diary. It was a practice that would become her musical trademark and endear her to legions of fans.

||||||||||||||||||||||||||||||||||||||||||||||||||

A RELATABLE STAR

It's hard to believe five feet eleven inches (1.8 m) Swift, who in 2008 the *New York Times* called "the

NO HOLDING BACK ||||||||||||||||||||||||||||||||||||||||||||||||||||||||||||||||||

Swift flashes back to her lonely middle school days in the song "The Outside" from her first album, *Taylor Swift*:

"So how can I ever try to be better?

Nobody ever lets me in

I can still see you, this ain't the best view

On the outside looking in"[3]

Growing up, Swift felt like an outsider at school.

most remarkable country music breakthrough artist of the decade," didn't have many friends in middle school or ever had problems with boys.[4] But it is her struggles with friends and love and relationships that make her seem so real to her fans. Swift may have become a superstar, but she was also the girl who didn't get invited to the best parties and the girl with a rotten boyfriend who cheated on her. She uses these life events as inspiration for her music, making her songs personal, yet universal.

> "I write songs about my adventures and misadventures, most of which concern love. Love is a tricky business. But if it wasn't, I wouldn't be so enthralled with it."[6]
>
> —TAYLOR SWIFT

Another intriguing trademark of Swift's songwriting is she is not afraid to name names. Many of her songs are about people she feels have done her wrong. That means the guy who cheated on her might hear his name in one of her songs played over and over again on the radio. The mean girls who rejected her at school can see themselves portrayed onscreen in her latest music video. "If you're horrible to me I'm going to write a song about you and you are not going to like it. That's how I operate," she told the *Daily Mail*.[5] But even Swift's revenge-streaked songs are relatable to her fans. Rather than coming off as mean–spirited, they're

Swift is known for writing songs about real people who have impacted her life.

"motivated by vulnerability and woundedness," noted one critic.[7]

Swift has lived her life as a celebrity openly and welcomes people to get to know her. She connects with fans online via her Web site, Facebook, Twitter, and YouTube. She also reaches them through sold-out concerts, TV and movie appearances, and countless interviews. But other than stories about a few high-profile romantic relationships, fans won't often find lurid stories about Swift in the tabloids. Her no-drinking, no-partying, clean-living lifestyle hasn't

FIRSTS

Since releasing her first single in 2006, Swift has achieved numerous recording-industry firsts. She was the first female artist in country music history to write or cowrite every song on a debut album selling more than 1 million copies. As of 2011, she was the youngest country artist to reach Number 1 with a self-written song and the youngest person and first female solo country artist to win the Grammy Award for Album of the Year. In 2010, Swift was the first artist to have two albums (*Taylor Swift* and *Fearless*) among one year's top ten sellers. In 2009, she was the most-played artist on the radio, and as of 2011, she was the top digital-selling artist of all time.

Swift tries to have an open relationship with her fans. She is active on social media and connects with her fans in whatever way she can.

garnered headlines the way some other young celebrities have.

Given her sweet-girl image, it may not come as a surprise Swift spent her childhood on a Christmas tree farm.

||||||||||

Taylor's mother, Andrea, has been supportive of Taylor throughout her music career.

CHAPTER 2

Growing Up Taylor

||||||||||||||||||||||||||||||||||

T aylor Alison Swift was born December 13, 1989, in Reading, Pennsylvania, and spent most of her childhood in Wyomissing, Pennsylvania, a small town outside of Reading. Her father, Scott, was a stockbroker who operated a Christmas tree farm as a hobby. Her mother, Andrea, stayed at home with Taylor and Austin, Taylor's younger brother by three years. Taylor loved growing up on the

Christmas tree farm, where there were fields to run through and horses to ride. One of her chores was searching for and removing praying mantis eggs from the Christmas trees, so the eggs would not hatch when people got their trees home.

||||||||||||||||||||||||||||||||||||||||||||||||||||||||||||

AN EARLY LOVE OF MUSIC

Taylor was surrounded by music from a very young age. Her mom was a fan of the rock-and-roll group Def Leppard and played their music while she was pregnant with Taylor. Marjorie Finlay, Taylor's grandmother, was an opera singer who sang around the house and in church on Sundays. When Taylor walked out of a Disney movie at age four having memorized the lyrics to every song, it was the music she remembered about the movie more than the plot.

Taylor was especially drawn to country music. After watching country singer Faith Hill's music video for "This Kiss" on television when she was nine years old, Taylor couldn't get the song out of her head. She knew she wanted to be a country singer. But even though music was all Taylor thought about and all she wanted to do, she figured she'd follow in her father's footsteps and become a stockbroker.

"[My] interest in music soon drew me to country music. I was infatuated with the sound, with the storytelling. I could relate to it. I can't really tell you why. With me, it was just instinctual."[1]

—TAYLOR SWIFT

Taylor showed early talent in writing and acting. As a fourth grader, she won a national poetry contest with a three-page poem titled "Monster in My Closet." She joined Berks Youth Theatre Academy, a children's theater troupe, and got lead roles in productions such as *Bye Bye Birdie*, because, as she would later recall in an interview for her hometown newspaper, she was the tallest member of the cast.

Even more than acting, Taylor loved the karaoke machine at the theater troupe's cast parties. Singing country music on the karaoke machine became one of her favorite things to do. She sang the songs of her favorite country artists,

Taylor was inspired by artists such as LeAnn Rimes, who was also a teenager when her first big hit was released.

including the Dixie Chicks and Shania Twain. The song "Blue," by LeAnn Rimes, who was only 14 years old at the time and doing all the things

Taylor dreamed of one day doing herself, especially inspired Taylor.

When she was ten, Taylor learned there was a weekly karaoke contest at the Pat Garrett Roadhouse in Strausstown, Pennsylvania, a nearby town. She sang there every week for more than a year until she won. Encouraged by her success, Taylor explored ways to get herself in front of larger groups of people. She sang the national anthem wherever she could, including at a Philadelphia 76ers game and the US Open tennis tournament in 2000.

> All the girls at school were going to sleepovers and breaking into their parents' liquor cabinets at the weekend, and all I wanted to do was go to festivals and sing karaoke music."[2]
>
> —TAYLOR SWIFT

When Taylor saw a TV special about country singer Faith Hill, who said she got her start when she moved to Nashville, Tennessee, Taylor realized if she wanted a career in country music there

Nashville, Tennessee, is considered the home of country music.

was only one place to be. She begged her parents to take her to Nashville, and in 2001 the family planned a trip.

SPRING BREAK IN NASHVILLE

Over her spring break in 2001, 11-year-old Taylor and her family took a trip to Tennessee to visit record label companies along Music Row in Nashville. Taylor was determined to visit as many recording companies as she could. She went into each company to introduce herself and drop off a demo CD. The CD featured her singing songs by Dolly Parton, the Dixie Chicks, and LeAnn Rimes.

"I was obsessively, obnoxiously bugging my parents every day—'We've got to go to Nashville. Can we go to Nashville? Can we go on a trip to Nashville like now? Or maybe spring break, can we go to Nashville?' Everything led to that. It was like, 'So how was your day at school today, Taylor?' 'Great. Can we go to Nashville?' I would bug them every day about it until finally we planned a trip to Nashville."[4]

—TAYLOR SWIFT

Taylor ran into each building, handed the CD to the receptionist while introducing herself, and left. "I thought they might be like, 'Oh, cool, you want a record deal? Here you go. Sign right there,'" she later told *CMT Insider*.[3]

The receptionists were very nice, Taylor recalled, but her cold calls didn't result in a record

Just a few blocks from Nashville's business district is a ten-block area of houses known as Music Row. The area was once a residential neighborhood. Now the houses and some newer buildings belong to recording studios, record companies, music publishing companies, management companies, and other businesses involved in the music industry.

While Nashville, also known as Music City, and Music Row have long been the hub of country music, rock-and-roll artists such as Bob Dylan and Elvis Presley have also recorded there. This city is home to major multinational recording companies, including Warner Bros., Mercury, BMG, MCA, Sony, Disney, and their smaller labels.

deal. The trip did give her a chance to check out Nashville, though. It was a huge city compared to Wyomissing, and thousands of people in Nashville wanted exactly what she did—a career in country music. However, what Taylor heard over and over again from country music insiders was Nashville was wary of young artists. This was because most of the people who listened to country and western radio were middle-aged women who liked older singers. Young performers were not a good fit for that demographic.

Taylor started playing guitar when she was 12 years old.

This was hard for Taylor to believe, since she figured there must be lots of girls just like her who not only loved country music but also wanted songs directed at them. So rather than giving up, Taylor decided to work harder. While she knew how to sing and perform, she needed something more to help her stand out. For Taylor, that meant learning to play the guitar and writing her own songs.

According to Andrea Swift, her daughter never said she wanted to be famous or be a star or be rich. If she had, Swift told *Entertainment Weekly*, she would have suggested to Taylor that she was pursuing music for the wrong reasons. But as long as Taylor found happiness in writing songs, Swift felt good about her daughter's career choice.

SETTING HERSELF APART

When she was 12, Taylor started taking guitar lessons from a man who fixed her parents' computers. She practiced for hours every day until her fingers were raw, then taped her fingers and played some more. Now, rather than singing at karaoke bars or dragging around her clunky karaoke machine, she performed at coffeehouses, baseball games, Boy Scout meetings, or any other venue where she could take her guitar and plug it into an amplifier. The more she performed, the more her skills improved, and the more people got a chance to hear her songs and her voice.

It was becoming obvious to Andrea and Scott Swift that their daughter's talent and enthusiasm for music was genuine. Taylor and her family began traveling to Nashville every couple of months, trying to meet with songwriters and anyone else in the business who could help Taylor get her foot in the door. In 2003, at age 13, she landed a meeting with RCA Records. After playing them approximately 20 songs, they were impressed and offered her a contract. Taylor was thrilled. One of the biggest record labels in Nashville wanted to sign her.

Even though the Christmas tree farm had been a great place to grow up, people in the music business were taking Taylor's talent seriously, and she was ready to move to Nashville. The family decided her career was worth the effort. Taylor's father transferred his work to Nashville, and in 2004 the family made the move to Hendersonville, Tennessee, a suburb of Nashville. The move would prove to be a very wise decision.

||||||||||

Taylor's music career took off when her family moved to Nashville.

CHAPTER 3

Taking on Nashville

||||||||||||||||||||||||||||||||||||||||||||||||||

The summer before Taylor's freshman year of high school, she and her family made the big move from Pennsylvania to a house overlooking a lake in Hendersonville, a town just outside of Nashville. Taylor attended Hendersonville High School for her freshman and sophomore years. She found high school a little more welcoming than middle school and made a few friends. She used the emotional

29

Taylor's social life fared better at her new school in Hendersonville than it had in Pennsylvania.

drama at school, such as a friend going through a breakup or guys being immature, as inspiration for her songwriting. She was a good student, with a 4.0 grade point average.

But Taylor was still tall and gangly and not very popular. She told *Rolling Stone* in a 2009 interview, "I was the girl who didn't get invited to parties, but if I did happen to go, you know, no one would throw a bottle at my head."[1]

||||||||||||||||||||||||||||||||||||||||||||||||||||||

BREAKS LOST AND GAINED

The contract with RCA didn't turn out the way Taylor had hoped. It was a development deal, which meant rather than immediately making records, RCA wanted to spend a year or two helping the young singer hone her talent. After making demos of songs other people had written, RCA might possibly make an album, but not until she was 18. This didn't make sense to Taylor, and she decided not to renew the contract.

But another big break was soon to come. While singing at a Broadcast Music, Inc. (BMI) showcase in 2004, Taylor was noticed by Arthur Buenahora, senior director of creative services and production at Sony/ATV Tree Music Publishing. He signed her to a songwriting contract. At age 15, Taylor was the youngest person the company had ever hired. Every day after school, Taylor would go to writing appointments at one of Nashville's many music studios. She came prepared with five to ten solid song ideas. "I wanted them to look at me as a person they were writing with, not a little kid," she told the *New York Times*.[2]

Like RCA, Buenahora had concerns about Taylor's youth. He noted in a *Billboard* interview the difficulty of convincing experienced songwriters Taylor could carry her own weight in writing sessions. He looked for writers who would listen to Taylor as well as mentor her. He paired her with songwriting veterans such as Brett Beavers, Scooter Carusoe, and the Warren Brothers. With the help of these veterans, Taylor wrote and stockpiled songs she and Buenahora could choose from to record later.

It wasn't long before Taylor had her next huge break. While singing at a showcase at the Bluebird Cafe in Nashville in 2005, she caught the attention of music-industry veteran Scott Borchetta, a former executive with Universal Records. He was starting a new record label and invited Taylor to join him. Although signing with an unproven company was risky, it was an attractive offer, partly because it was not a development deal. Taylor recalled in a 2009 interview,

I knew that he would not try to make me something that I didn't want to be, play some character that I wasn't, fit some mold. But it was still a leap of faith. . . [3]

She signed with Borchetta to the unnamed label that would become Big Machine Records.

In August 2005, Taylor played a song for Borchetta she had written during a freshman math class. She had titled the song, "When You Think Tim McGraw." The song is about two people who fall in love listening to a Tim McGraw tune, break up, and then are reminded of each other whenever they hear the song. Borchetta was so impressed with the song's potential, he called it "a grenade in a still pond."[4]

|||||||||||||||||||||||||||||||||||||||||||||||||||||||||

A MILLION WAYS IT COULD HAVE GONE WRONG

|||||||||||||||||||||||||

On NBC's *Dateline*, Taylor discussed her first conversation with Borchetta, when he asked if she wanted to sign onto his new record label. She said,

"[H]e didn't have a name for it. He didn't have a building for it. And he didn't have a staff for it. But he had a dream, and would I go on board. I went with my gut instinct which. . . just said, 'say yes.' There are a million ways it could've gone wrong."[5]

Country singer Tim McGraw was the inspiration
behind Taylor's first big hit.

"TIM McGRAW"

Although Borchetta thought the single could be a
hit, he wasn't sure if country radio would accept

Taylor's young sound. He took advantage of Taylor's already-existing MySpace page and Web site in order to attract young fans. He also created a series of short, biographical videos that aired on the Great American Country (GAC) cable network. There was a buzz around Taylor before her song was ever released. When Big Machine Records released the newly titled "Tim McGraw" on June 19, 2006, people were curious about the new artist.

Taylor stuffed promotional CDs of her song into envelopes destined for radio stations, giving each CD the mental message, "Please, please just listen

NEW COUNTRY TERRITORY—ONLINE

Borchetta and other music-industry insiders attributed part of the success of Taylor's first album to the Internet. Soon after signing her, Borchetta and Taylor set out to build a grassroots online following for the singer, with the goal of going viral. She gained a huge following on her MySpace page, especially with younger, computer-savvy fans who spread the word and helped make her seem more legitimate to country radio stations hesitant to play a young, new, female artist.

By August 2007, Taylor had tallied 20.9 million views on her MySpace page, and she reported spending time each day following up with her MySpace fans. Today, Taylor continues to connect with her fans via Facebook and her Twitter feed.

to this one time."[6] She crisscrossed the country on an eight-week radio station tour promoting the single, living in hotel rooms, and sometimes sleeping in the backseats of rental cars. Her mom once drove her to three different cities in one day.

Taylor's and the record company's efforts paid off. "Tim McGraw" peaked at Number 14 on the *Billboard* country chart, successfully reaching an audience unfamiliar to traditional Nashville— teenage girls. The time was right to release Taylor's first album.

‖‖‖

TAYLOR SWIFT

Taylor's first album, *Taylor Swift*, was released on October 24, 2006. Taylor wrote or cowrote every song on the 11-track album. She had written one song, "The Outside,"—about her middle school experience with the mean girls— when she was only 12. Liz Rose, cowriter with Taylor on seven songs, told the Associated Press about her young partner, "She's a genius, coming in with ideas and a melody. She'd come in and write with this old lady, and I'd never second-guess her. I respect her a lot."[7]

Scott Borchetta's label, Big Machine Records, produced Taylor's first album.

In addition to "Tim McGraw" and "The Outside," all the tracks on the album are emotional and personal. "Picture to Burn" and "Should've Said

No" are songs about boys she was angry with. "Tied Together with a Smile" is about a girl Taylor knew with an eating disorder. The album ends with "Our Song," a song about a couple who doesn't have a song. Taylor wrote the song in 15 minutes for a ninth-grade talent show. Taylor explains on her Web site that she placed it as the last track because of the hint in the chorus's lyrics: "play it again."[8]

The album sold a modest 39,000 copies in its first week, but kept selling as Taylor and Big Machine Records released more singles that turned into hits. "Teardrops on My Guitar," a song about Taylor's unrequited high school crush, Drew, landed at Number 2 on the *Billboard* Hot Country Singles chart. The song became a crossover hit when it peaked at Number 13 on the *Billboard* Hot 100. Pop radio stations in many cities were willing to play the song once it had reached high enough in the country market.

After 39 weeks, *Taylor Swift* finally reached the top of *Billboard's* Top Country Albums chart. The last time an artist had taken so long to reach the top spot was the Dixie Chicks's album *Fly*, after 51 weeks in 1999. In addition to going multiplatinum, the album would eventually land five singles in the

While performers who cross over from rap or indie to pop don't usually raise eyebrows, country-to-pop crossovers have been known to fail. Nashville can be protective and possessive of its own sound. That's why Taylor and Borchetta are both concerned about keeping Taylor's music true to her country roots instead of trying to chase pop radio. According to Borchetta in 2008, country radio would always get Taylor's singles first and would always be first in line at meet-and-greets.

top ten on the *Billboard* Top 40 and two Number 1 singles on the *Billboard* country chart.

With her album and singles climbing the charts, Taylor would be tapped by established country acts to join their tours. It was time for her to hit the road.

|||||||||||

Taylor's first tour experience came in 2006, when she opened for Rascal Flatts.

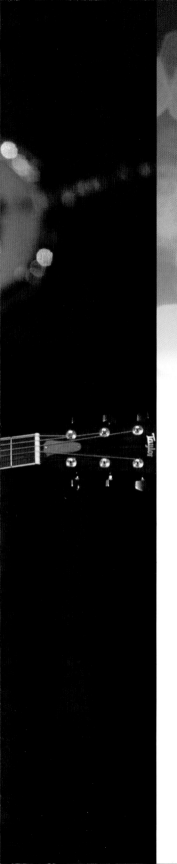

CHAPTER 4

Opening Act: On the Road

||||||||||||||||||||||||||||||||||||||||||||||||||||||||||||||||||||||||

Even before Taylor released her first album in October 2006, country trio Rascal Flatts asked the 16-year-old to join their concert tour. Rascal Flatts's original opening act, country singer Eric Church, had been fired from the tour. Taylor took his place for the tour's last nine dates beginning on October 19, 2006. She would have been a junior at Hendersonville High School that fall, but touring made it impossible for her to attend school. Instead, she was homeschooled for her junior and senior years through the Aaron Academy, a private Christian school.

As she was wrapping up her tour with Rascal Flatts, Taylor was invited to open for country superstar George Strait's winter tour, along with country veteran Ronnie Milsap. Even though it meant she would go from one tour to another without much of a break, Taylor would have the opportunity to perform with country music legends. She told Country Music Television (CMT) in an interview, "You couldn't pay me enough money to go back [home]. . . . I'm having a blast right now. I feel like this is what I'm wired for."[1]

A WONDERFUL CAREER AHEAD OF HER

Reporter Bobbi Smith had this to say about then 16-year-old Taylor's opening act for Rascal Flatts in Toronto on November 1, 2006:

> "She had a bright smile and seemed absolutely thrilled to be on that stage. . . . She talked between songs and took command of the stage with ease. . . . The brief set seemed to fly by and after closing with a fun upbeat tune called 'Picture to Burn,' Taylor was gone. I was definitely impressed by this young woman, and I think she's going to have a wonderful career ahead of her."[2]

It's not unusual for performers to prank each other while onstage. As Brad Paisley sang "I'm Gonna Miss Her," his hit song about fishing, Swift sauntered onstage wearing waders and a fishing hat. She threw stuffed fish and plastic worms into the audience and reeled a giant stuffed fish onto the stage with a fishing pole.

At the end of Swift's 2008 tour with Rascal Flatts, all the band members joined Swift onstage after her last song—dressed as Swift, in short dresses and blond wigs.

Her 15-minute set included her single "Tim McGraw" and the song "Teardrops on My Guitar," which would become another major hit single from her album. Taylor celebrated her seventeenth birthday in December, and the tour kicked off in Louisiana in January.

After her tour with Strait wrapped up in March, Taylor began another tour from April through June 2007, this time with country star Brad Paisley. She shared opening duties with country star Jack Ingram and former *American Idol* contestant Kellie Pickler, with whom Taylor became good friends. Then, over the summer of 2007, Taylor was an opening act for the Soul2Soul Tour with country superstars Faith Hill and Tim McGraw—the inspiration for Taylor's first hit single.

Taylor seemed poised for superstardom, a position recognized by the Country Music Association (CMA), which honored Taylor in November 2007 with its Horizon Award for best new artist. In her tearful and exuberant acceptance speech, Taylor joked that receiving the award was the highlight of her senior year.

||||||||||||||||||||||||||||||||||||||||||||||||||||||||||

TURNING 18

Swift turned 18 on December 13, 2007. The day started quietly with Swift at the computer, still in her pajamas, registering to vote. That night, her parents hosted a birthday party at a Nashville

SWIFT MEETS HER INSPIRATION ||||||||||||||||||||||||||||||||||||||||||

Taylor did not win an award at the 2007 Academy of Country Music (ACM) Awards. But she did get to meet her inspiration, McGraw, for the first time. After performing a song for the awards show, she walked over to McGraw and his wife, Faith Hill, and introduced herself. McGraw and Swift hugged, which prompted the ACM Award's host, country singer Reba McEntire, to invite any teenage boys to write a song about her.

Taylor finally met McGraw and his wife, Hill, in 2007.

dance club. The 200 guests included her friend
Pickler, country stars John Rich and Chuck Wicks,
and the country group Lady Antebellum.
Borchetta handed Swift the keys to her birthday

Swift was nominated for her first Grammy in 2007,
for the award of Best New Artist.

present—a pink truck that happened to match the
color of her dress.

Another birthday present was Swift's nomination in December 2007 for a Grammy Award as Best New Artist. Although she did not win the award, Swift appeared excited and overwhelmed at the nomination ceremony, fighting back tears and hugging the more subdued performers sitting next to her.

||||||||||||||||||||||||||||||||||||||||||||||||||||||||||||||

SWIFT SUCCESS

Also that December, a little more than a year after its release, *Taylor Swift* had gone double platinum, selling 2.5 million copies. Three of the album's singles reached the top ten on *Billboard*'s Hot Country Songs chart, including "Our Song," which spent six weeks at Number 1. In addition to its

SWIFT AND PICKLER: BFFs ||||||||||||||||||||||||||||||||||||||||||||||||||

Even though Pickler is older than Swift by four years, she refers to Swift as her big sister. "I'm obnoxious and immature. . . . She's reserved and well put-together. She keeps me in line." In return, Swift said of Pickler, "She will never tell you something she doesn't mean. I respect that, and . . . the fact that she came from a situation where she wasn't given much and made the most of her life."[3] According to Pickler, that sense of sisterhood has also been helped by the way Swift's parents have taken good care of her on the road.

country success, the album was one of the ten best-selling pop albums of 2007.

Swift's MySpace page hit 41 million song listens, and the rising star was becoming popular on television. Her "Our Song" music video spent a record seven weeks at the Number 1 spot on CMT. Her "Teardrops on My Guitar" video found its way onto Music Television (MTV), a network that rarely played country music. Swift would even appear live on the MTV afternoon program *Total Request Live*.

Some close to Swift worried her success was coming too quickly. In a February 2008 *Washington Post* interview, Borchetta said he was afraid by the time she turned 19, Swift would reach all her goals and burn out. But given Swift's current energy and enthusiasm for every part of her career, that didn't seem to be a problem.

||||||||||||||||||||||||||||||||||||||||||||||||||||||||||

SLOW ROMANCE

There was one area of Swift's life moving at a slower speed than her music career. Even though she loved writing songs about boys and love

In 2008, Swift was focusing on making another album rather than looking for a romantic relationship.

and romance, in a 2008 interview she claimed she hadn't kissed a boy in two years. She told interviewers she wasn't actively looking for a romantic relationship and, for now, music was her boyfriend. Plus, her history of writing songs about guys who broke her heart probably kept anyone from asking her out, fearing she would pen a song about them. With her huge following of fans, she'd hear from them if they didn't approve of the guy

> "I'm not going to try to act like some adult who has it all together and isn't fazed at all by that. I am. I'm completely affected by it. I don't like it when people who are young act like they're 40. . . . Some people might say I'm mature for my age, but it's not something I'm trying to do, you know? I'm just me."[4]
>
> —TAYLOR SWIFT

she chose, which meant she had to find someone nice. The timing was right to focus on music instead of a relationship.

GOING PLATINUM

Gold, platinum, multi-platinum, and diamond are all music awards based on a record's sales. They are certified by the Recording Industry Association of America (RIAA), a music trade organization. Gold represents sales of 500,000 copies, platinum 1 million copies, and diamond 10 million copies. Multiplatinum means an album has reached platinum two or more times. Perry Como received the first gold plaque in 1958 for his hit single "Catch a Falling Star."

The first platinum for an album was awarded to The Eagles's *Their Greatest Hits 1971–1975*, which was the best-selling album of the twentieth century.

Swift was crowned the RIAA's top certified artist of digital singles spanning the decade 2000 to 2009. In 2011, she made digital gold and platinum program history with 22.5 million career digital certifications. As of April 2011, all of Swift's albums and three of her singles were certified multiplatinum.

By March 2008, Swift had finished recording six songs for her second album, she was getting ready to record six more, and she had a third recording session scheduled for the summer. She wanted a lot of songs to choose from. Swift had much to look forward to over the rest of 2008, in addition to a new album: more touring, more awards, higher record sales . . . and finally, romance.

Swift got the chance to perform with her mother's favorite band, Def Leppard, in 2008.

CHAPTER 5

Fearless

|||||||||||||||||||||||||||||||||||||||||||||||||

As Swift's fame grew, her opportunities expanded beyond singing and songwriting. In 2008, Swift was getting into acting and merchandising. She continued racking up award nominations and went on a second tour with Rascal Flatts, all while completing her senior year of high school and readying her next album for a November release.

||||||||||||||||||||||||||||||||

NEW OPPORTUNITIES

Swift filmed a number of television and movie appearances in 2008. In a documentary for the CMT *Crossroads* performance series, Swift fulfilled her childhood dream of performing with Def Leppard, her mother's favorite band. In April, Swift filmed a documentary for the MTV series *Once Upon a Prom*, where she attended a high school prom in Tuscaloosa, Alabama. Also in 2008, she had cameo appearances with singing trio the Jonas Brothers in their Disney concert film, *Jonas Brothers: The 3D Concert Experience*, which was released in 2009. She also appeared in the Disney film *Hannah Montana: The Movie*.

SENIOR PROM

Homeschooling and scheduling conflicts kept Swift from attending senior prom at her former high school, Hendersonville High, but that didn't keep her from going to a prom. As part of MTV's *Once Upon a Prom* series, she went to the prom at Hillcrest High School in Tuscaloosa. The school was chosen by MTV, but Swift selected her date, senior Whit Wright, from approximately 50 boys who had applied. He bought her a wrist corsage, and Swift told *People* magazine she had a great time; she felt like she was in high school again, in a good way, without the drama.

Swift was drenched with water as she performed at the 2008 ACM awards. She took home three awards that night.

On April 14, 2008, Swift won two fan-voted CMT awards, Female Video of the Year and overall Video of the Year, for her video "Our Song." She accepted both awards barefoot because her feet hurt. At the ACM awards on May 8, she won the award for Top New Female Vocalist and was drenched with water from onstage raindrops as she performed "Should've Said No."

In June 2008, Swift was on the road again with Rascal Flatts, opening for its Bob That Head Tour, which would run the rest of the summer, hitting more than 30 US cities before it finished in September.

Swift also had recorded and released two EPs, or extended-play CDs, between her first and second albums. *Sounds of the Season: The Taylor Swift Holiday Collection* released on October 14, 2007, and *Beautiful Eyes*, a CD and DVD limited-edition set released on July 15, 2008. During her busy year, she also managed to graduate. In July 2008, Swift received her high school diploma from the Aaron Academy.

||||||||||||||||||||||||||||||||||||||||||||||||||||||||||||

ROCKY ROMANCE

In August 2008, rumors swirled that Swift was dating heartthrob Joe Jonas of the Jonas Brothers. In July, she had shot a guest spot for their Disney concert movie, and Jonas was seen at Swift's

Swift dated musician Joe Jonas for a few months in 2008.
She went on to write a song about him on her new album.

concert performance in Florida sitting next to her
dad and then backstage after her set was finished.
While admitting that Jonas was a friend and an
amazing guy, Swift laughed off the rumors that they
were an item.

Then in October, before they had publicly announced they were a couple, Swift admitted to the relationship in an appearance on *The Ellen DeGeneres Show*. She told DeGeneres he'd broken up with her over the phone in 25 seconds for another girl, actress Camilla Belle. However, Swift would have plenty to take her mind off the breakup.

In November, Swift's song "Teardrops on My Guitar" won the BMI Country Song of the Year award, and she performed at the CMA and American Music Academy (AMA) Awards shows. While Swift did not win a CMA award, she won for Country Favorite Female Artist at the AMAs.

That fall, Swift used her celebrity status to get into merchandising. She had a line of fashion dolls, and she released a line of clothing with the company l.e.i., to be sold at Walmart stores. But Swift's fans were clamoring for new music. It had been two years since she'd released her first full album, and her fans, known as the Taylor Nation, were looking forward to more songs from their favorite star. She wouldn't disappoint them.

SWIFT'S SOPHOMORE ALBUM

Swift's second full album, *Fearless*, was released November 11, 2008. She was still 18 and had been writing songs nonstop, claiming to have written 500 songs by then, a fifth of which she considered for *Fearless*. On her Web site, Swift explained the title didn't mean the "absence of fear," but rather the idea of having fear, but living through it and moving on.[1]

Swift wrote seven songs on the 13-track album and cowrote the other six. They're a continuation of Swift's favorite diary-entry themes from her first album: love, boys, and relationships—just the topics her fans related to. "Love Story," which Swift

UNOFFICIAL SNEAK PEAK

Before the official release of *Fearless*, nearly 100 people (mostly teenage girls) posted videos of themselves performing the title track on YouTube. The music had been leaked when a radio station shot a video of Swift singing the song for guests on a tour bus in 2007. Someone posted the music on the Internet, and girls began making videos of themselves singing the song in their bedrooms. The unauthorized videos infringed on copyright laws, but Swift found the attention flattering. Nonetheless, as a result of the slipup, Swift's managers stopped allowing her to play new music before it was released.

wrote on her bedroom floor, is about a boy Swift wanted to date, whom her parents and friends didn't approve of. The situation reminded Swift of Shakespeare's play *Romeo and Juliet*, and she used part of the plot for the song's storyline. In "You Belong With Me," Swift tries to persuade a boy to come to his senses and fall for her girl-next-door charms. Swift reflects back on high school angst in "Fifteen," and "Hey Stephen" is about a guy who doesn't know she likes him. In "Forever and Always," a song Swift wrote and recorded just before the album's release, she alludes to her breakup with Jonas.

While her debut album, *Taylor Swift*, was a huge success in the world of country music, *Fearless* made Swift the biggest star of 2008 in any musical genre. The album went gold in its first week and, combined with sales of her first album, made Swift

RADIO-READY CHARMERS |||||||||||||||||||||||||||||||||||||||||||||||||||||||||||||

Chris Richards, a music critic for the *Washington Post*, said of Swift's second album,

"In Swift's world, every song is a radio-ready charmer, confirming the 18-year-old's ability to pen a gaggle of consistently pleasing tunes. . . . Swift sounds like she's genuinely singing to the hallways of her high school."[2]

Swift's *Fearless* was an international hit and did well with both pop and country audiences.

the highest-grossing artist of the year. Not a bad way to celebrate her nineteenth birthday. With her star rising quickly, Swift had one major goal she still had not reached: headlining her own tour.

‖‖‖‖‖‖‖‖

In 2009, Swift went on her Fearless Tour, her first tour as the headliner.

CHAPTER 6

Headliner at Last

||||||||||||||||||||||||||||||||||||||||

On January 30, 2009, Swift, who had just turned 19, announced that her Fearless Tour would kick off on April 23, in Evansville, Indiana. It would then hit 51 other cities over the following six months. The country music group Gloriana would be joining her along with Pickler as Swift's opening acts. All 52 shows quickly sold out. The Staples Center in Los Angeles, California, ran out of tickets in two minutes. Madison Square Garden in New York City sold out in one minute. "Throughout my whole career, I've never seen anything like this," Swift's tour promoter, Louie Messina, told *Dateline*. "As Bruce Springsteen was the voice of his generation, Taylor is the voice of her generation."[1]

Three weeks prior to the Evansville opening, Swift and her crew rehearsed in a rented warehouse in Nashville, where they set up the entire stage. Swift had been opening for other acts since she was 16 and had spent a few years sitting in tour buses at night, thinking about what she'd do onstage. Now, still a teenager, she was calling the shots of every performance detail, from set design— including a castle that acted as a huge projector screen, hidden elevator, and collapsible turret—to

SWIFT ON *CSI*

In January 2009, Swift filmed an episode of the CBS television crime drama *CSI: Crime Scene Investigation*. The episode, which aired on March 5, features Swift as a Las Vegas, Nevada, hotel manager's daughter. Swift's character, Hayley, gets in trouble and is murdered. Although Swift doesn't have many lines, she appears in flashbacks throughout the episode and dyed her hair brown for the part.

When Swift was 16 years old and playing at the Wildhorse Saloon in Nashville, she was impressed by 12 screaming girls wearing Taylor Swift shirts and face paint, as if they were at a football game. Her mom brought the girls backstage, and they told Swift they had driven all the way from Evansville, Indiana, to see her play. After that, Swift always had a good feeling whenever she thought of Evansville. When given options on where to start her tour, it was an easy choice.

choosing the backup dancers. She decided which songs she would play and how her band would perform them. And she continued tweaking the show after the tour started.

With added dates, Swift would end up spending the rest of 2009 and part of 2010 on the road with the Fearless Tour. She would also spend time in 2009 attending a slew of award shows, sometimes via satellite.

MORE AWARDS

In 2009, "You Belong with Me" peaked at Number 2 on the pop charts, cementing Swift's status as a crossover artist. Topping the 2009 sales charts, *Fearless* went multiplatinum, selling 3.2 million copies. Fans downloaded another 12 million tracks. Among her many awards in 2009, *Fearless* would garner Album of the Year awards from three different music organizations: the Grammys, the ACM awards, and the CMA awards.

In spite of her growing fame, a portion of the public was still unfamiliar with the country-pop star. However, that would change with Swift's

> "Taylor's a 40-year-old in a 19-year-old's body. She's made and meant to be doing what she's doing. She knows how to lead the room and lead the stage. And she knows how to do it too without being some taskmaster."[2]
>
> —*CAITLIN EVANSON, FIDDLER, DATELINE, MAY 2009*

acceptance of the award for Best Female Video at the MTV Video Music Awards (VMAs)—it would become one of the biggest celebrity news stories of 2009.

GRAMMY AWARDS

Fearless won album of the year at the 2009 Grammy Awards.

Swift appeared stunned when West interrupted
her VMA acceptance speech.

CELEBRITY FEUD

On September 13, a thrilled Swift walked across
the Radio City Music Hall stage to accept the
statuette for Best Female Video during MTV's VMA

show, for her video "You Belong with Me." She had just begun her acceptance speech when rap singer Kanye West bounded onto the stage, grabbed the microphone from her hand, and announced that R & B singer Beyoncé deserved the award.

"Yo Taylor," he said to Swift and the audience, "I'm really happy for you, I'll let you finish, but Beyoncé has one of the best videos of all time. One of the best videos of all time!"[3]

Cameras panned over the stunned audience and horrified Beyoncé. By the time West finished his outburst, Swift's time at the podium was up. The crowd gave Swift a standing ovation, and when Beyoncé later accepted her award for Video of the Year, she invited Swift onstage to finish her speech. West was tossed from the awards show

SWIFT'S GRAMMYS |||||||||||||||||||||||||||||||||||||||||||||||||||||||||||||

As of 2011, *Fearless* was the most-awarded album in the history of country music. In addition to numerous awards from BMI and *Billboard*, Swift and her album won four Grammys at the 2010 Grammy Awards for her work in 2009. Swift's 2010 Grammys were Album of the Year for *Fearless*, Best Country Album for *Fearless*, Best Female Country Vocal Performance for her song "White Horse," and Best Country Song for "White Horse."

Swift finished her VMA acceptance speech during Beyoncé's acceptance of the award for Video of the Year.

and later apologized on his blog. Swift said of the event,

> I was standing on stage and I was really excited because I'd just won the award. And then I was really excited because Kanye West was on the stage. And then, I wasn't excited anymore after that.[4]

After Swift described her feelings about the incident on the TV talk show *The View* a few days later, West called her and apologized. She accepted his apology and, in typical Swift style, would go on to write two songs about him, although not the songs everyone expected.

||||||||||||

Swift opened her *Saturday Night Live* monologue with a song when she hosted the show in 2009.

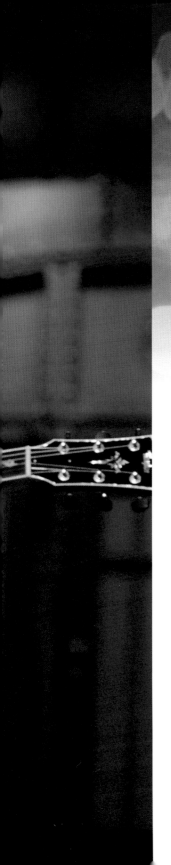

CHAPTER 7
Love and Music

||||||||||||||||||||||||||||||||||||||||||||||||||||||||||||||||||||||||||||||||||||||||||

Swift's incident with West at the September 2009 MTV VMAs show took on the status of a celebrity mega-feud. On November 7, two months after the infamous stage storming, Swift was scheduled to host the late-night television comedy program *Saturday Night Live (SNL)*. Many people wondered if she would take the opportunity to publicly get back at West.

Swift's *SNL* monologue—which she wrote herself—was in the form of a song making fun of how she subtly mentions people in songs. In addition to bringing up her ex Jonas and her rumored current flame, actor Taylor Lautner, she gave West a gentle dig:

> *You might be expecting me to say something bad about Kanye*
>
> *And how he ran up on the stage and ruined my VMA monologue*
>
> *But there's nothing more to say, 'cuz everything's okay*
>
> *I've got security lining the stage[1]*

THE *SNL* "MONOLOGUE SONG"

In addition to Swift's dig at Kanye West in her *SNL* monologue, she had a few humorous lyrics for her ex-boyfriend Jonas:

"You might think I'd bring up Joe, that guy who broke up with me on the phone

But I'm not gonna mention him in my monologue

Hey, Joe! I'm doing real well! I'm hosting SNL!"

And she had this not-too cryptic message about Taylor Lautner:

"And if you're wondering if I might be dating the werewolf from Twilight..."

She then waved, mouthed "Hi, Taylor," and blew a kiss.[2]

Swift and Lautner were a couple for a short time in 2009, and she wrote a song about him on her new album.

While it wasn't the skewering some were expecting, Swift was praised for her *SNL* performance. One critic called her the best *SNL* host of the season. The episode also had the biggest audience of 2009, with 6.8 million viewers. It topped all the shows on television in prime time

Swift's first noncameo film role was in the 2010 movie *Valentine's Day*.

that Saturday among viewers between the ages of 18 and 45, and it rated better than any nonsport program on a Saturday night in almost three years.

GROWING UP

Whether Swift was crossing over from singing to acting was yet to be determined. But there was no denying that she was crossing over from teen to adult, and she had the romantic battle scars to prove it. Though Swift and Lautner never publicly admitted to a relationship, they were spotted hanging out together. But at the end of December 2009, after only three months of dating, a source told the entertainment magazine *Us Weekly* that the couple had amicably broken up.

By January 2010, Swift was 20 years old and seemed more centered in the tabloids' crosshairs than ever. Her domination at the Grammy Awards on January 31, in which she garnered four awards, including Album of the Year, was accompanied by widespread criticism of her off-key duet with singer Stevie Nicks. Even music-industry critics who had previously praised Swift were critical of her performance.

VALENTINES: FILMED AND REAL

Swift and Lautner met on the set of the romantic-comedy movie *Valentine's Day*, filmed in the summer of 2009. Swift had a minor role as Felicia, a girl forced to go to a high school gym class. Lautner, best known for his role as the werewolf Jacob in the *Twilight* movies, played the role of Willy, Felicia's boyfriend. Swift also wrote two songs for the movie: "Today Was a Fairytale" and "Jump Then Fall."

Scrutiny of Swift's work and personal life would only increase with Swift's further romances, although she would do her best to keep the relationships quiet—except in her songs.

IIIIIIIIIIIIIIIIIIIIIIIIIIIIIIIIIIIIIIIIIIIIIIIIIIIII

ARE THEY OR AREN'T THEY?

During 2010, Swift was romantically linked to a few men, starting with actor Cory Monteith, star of the television series *Glee*. Like Swift's other romances, the relationship was never confirmed. In May, blues-pop musician John Mayer joined Swift for a couple of concert duets in Los Angeles. They'd been seen together earlier in the year, but neither Swift nor Mayer admitted to a relationship. Then, over the summer, Swift was spotted in different locations with actor Toby Hemingway, the costar of a music video from her upcoming album. This fueled rumors the pair were an item—again unconfirmed.

Swift's romantic ties to actor Jake Gyllenhaal in the fall were slightly more public. The couple was seen together brunching with friends, holding hands, and eating ice cream. But by December, they had reportedly split up and were spending the holidays apart.

Swift and Mayer started dating after performing several duets together. Two songs from Swift's *Speak Now* album are rumored to be based on her relationship with Mayer.

If nothing else, Swift's failed romances and dealing with the perils of celebrity were providing her with rich material for her third studio album, which she'd been recording almost as soon as *Fearless* was released.

SPEAK NOW

Swift's album *Speak Now* was released October 25, 2010. Almost 21, Swift was no longer a teenager focused on the drama of high school hallways. The songs on the album—which she wrote entirely on her own—are still emotion-filled diary entries, but now they are up close and adult. According to Swift, the title of the album was inspired by the moment the preacher says, "Speak now or forever hold your peace," just before the wedding vows. It's the last chance for someone to protest and say what he or she may be keeping inside. Each of the album's songs is an open letter to a specific person or people—words Swift didn't say when the moment was right in front of her.[3]

Because Swift is largely vague about who her open letters are to, it's left to others to piece together the hints found in her lyrics and elsewhere, including statements on her Web site and random words she capitalizes in her lyric booklets. For example, the capitalized letters of

TITLE CHANGE

Borchetta of Big Machine Records told *Billboard* magazine that he and Swift originally titled her third album *Enchanted*. But after listening to a few of her new songs, Borchetta realized she wasn't writing about fairy tales and high school anymore, and he told her *Enchanted* just didn't fit. Swift excused herself from their conversation, and by the time she returned a few minutes later, she had the new title—*Speak Now*.

the "Enchanted" lyrics spell *A-D-A-M*, which many think is a reference to musician Adam Young of Owl City. Most people assume "Better than Revenge" is about Camilla Belle, the woman Jonas reportedly broke up with Swift to be with. Swift's anger and heartbreak are also found in a few other songs on the album, none more so than in "Dear John," most likely about ex-boyfriend Mayer.

One of the album's singles, "The Story of Us," is also assumed to be about Mayer, referring to the discomfort Swift felt when she nearly encountered him at the 2010 CMT Awards. "Mean" is about getting picked on and feeling powerless, most likely inspired by critic Bob Lefsetz. "Back to December" is Swift's first apology song and is likely for ex-boyfriend Lautner. The album also touches on other personal aspects of Swift's recent life, including a conciliatory scolding of West in her song "Innocent."

Would fans and critics connect with Swift's more mature collection of songs? It would take only days to find out.

||||||||||

Swift's *Speak Now* album was an instant success that she took on tour around the world in 2011.

CHAPTER 8

Forever and Always

||||||||||||||||||||||||||||||||||||||||||||

Fans definitely connected with *Speak Now*, Taylor Swift's third studio album. It went platinum in its first week of sales, the second-best week for a female artist since pop superstar Britney Spears's 2000 album, *Oops! I Did It Again*. Sales were helped by a massive advertising campaign from Target stores and the early release of the blockbuster single "Mine," which got heavy radio play and had sold more than 1 million downloads by the time Swift's album was released.

Critics and reviewers generally agreed that *Speak Now* was Swift's strongest album and showed she was naturally progressing from teen to adult without alienating her younger fans. Rob Sheffield wrote in *Rolling Stone* magazine, "Swift's third album, *Speak Now*, is roughly twice as good as 2008's *Fearless*, which was roughly twice as good as her 2006 debut."[1]

Jon Caramanica of the *New York Times* said,

Speak Now is . . . a bravura work of nontransparent transparency. . . . The great accomplishment of this album . . . is that Ms. Swift is at her most musically adventurous when she's most incensed.[2]

Swift had the opportunity to publicize her album during a Thanksgiving television special that aired November 25, 2010, on NBC. The hour-long program followed Swift performing songs from *Speak Now* in different settings, including New York's Central Park and Hollywood, California.

Life was moving quickly for Swift. She turned 21 on December 13, 2010, noting on her Web site, "I've apparently been the victim of growing up, which apparently happens to all of us at one point or another."[4] She had her own place now too. The previous summer, she had moved out of her parents' house into a midtown Nashville penthouse with barn-wood floors, brick walls, and mismatched furniture in the kitchen. And Swift

"People like to fixate on Taylor Swift's youth, as if to say, yeah, she's pretty good for her age. But that just begs the question: Where are all the older people who are supposedly making better pop records than Taylor Swift? There aren't any. In a mere four years, the 20-year-old Nashville firecracker has put her name on three dozen or so of the smartest songs released by anyone in pop, rock, or country."[5]

—*ROB SHEFFIELD*, ROLLING STONE, OCTOBER 2010

Swift's Speak Now Tour featured over-the-top elements, including a floating balcony and elaborate costumes.

Swift was having a rough day at one of her Speak Now Tour rehearsals, so she scrawled on her arm a lyric from a song by her friend, actress and pop singer Selena Gomez. The lyric read: "You've got every right to a beautiful life."[6] Swift thought it looked cool and started writing lyrics on her arm with a permanent marker before every North American performance. The words of Tom Petty, Faith Hill, the Dixie Chicks, and other artists have graced her arm. According to Swift, the lyrics are like a "mood ring."[7]

was busy working on another ambitious tour that would span the world and take up most of 2011.

||||||||||||||||||||||||||||||||||||||||||||||||||||

SPEAK NOW WORLD TOUR

In November 2010, Swift announced she would be taking *Speak Now* on the road in a new tour, beginning February 9, 2011. The tour would start in Singapore, with performances across Asia and Europe, and then it would hit the United States on May 27 in Omaha, Nebraska. The tour was scheduled to end in Dallas, Texas, on October 8, 2011, but with added dates and venues, the tour actually extended to November 22, 2011, in New

To unwind after her Fearless Tour and Speak Now Tour performances, Swift held a meet-and-greet called the T Party in a giant tent set up as a Moroccan living room. During her shows, Swift had people scour the audience for fans with the craziest outfits or little kids who sang along to all Swift's songs. They would then invite those fans to join her.

York City. The tour had approximately 100 shows, including eight stadium performances.

Like her Fearless Tour, Swift's new show featured a dramatic and spectacular set, including a descending staircase, a wedding chapel, and a floating balcony. The show had aerialists, dancers, fireworks, glow sticks for the audience, twinkling trees, a snowstorm, and nine costume changes—so many details that Swift admitted it was a mental challenge to remember all of them every night. She found inspiration for her sets from musicals such as *Wicked*. The costume designer from *Wicked* even created costumes for the Speak Now Tour.

Swift packed arenas and stadiums across the country, including the homes of the NFL's New England Patriots, Pittsburg Steelers, and

Detroit Lions. Noted a reviewer for the *New York Times*, "Through the set, as she ran through glamorous costume changes, hit her marks and telegraphed lyrics with finger-pointing gestures, her composure never faltered."[8] According to Swift, one of her most memorable performances was during an outdoor concert at Gillette Stadium in Massachusetts when she felt raindrops start to fall while singing "Fearless." A deluge of rain was

> "She's the full package, somebody who writes her own songs, and is so good at it, so smart; who sings, plays the guitar, looks as good as she looks, works that hard, is that engaging and so savvy. It's an extraordinary combination."[9]
>
> —SCOTT BORCHETTA, BIG MACHINE RECORDS

soon drenching her and the audience, but instead of leaving, as she feared they would, the audience simply danced in the rain and screamed louder.

Throughout the tour, Swift wove in surprise duets with other musicians, highlighting their music instead of her own. Her duet partners included pop artists Justin Bieber and Jason Mraz; hip-hop performers Nicki Minaj, Usher, and T. I.; and country stars Kenny Chesney and McGraw. She also covered songs by local artists, researching famous musicians from the areas she was performing. At a California concert, she sang "God Only Knows" by the Beach Boys and "Sweet Escape" by pop star and California native Gwen Stefani.

GIVING BACK

Over the course of her career, Swift has donated to or been active in a number of charitable causes. On September 17, 2007, she helped launch a campaign with Tennessee Governor Phil Bredesen to inform children about online predators. In January 2008, she gave her eighteenth-birthday pink pickup truck to a youth camp for children with serious medical conditions. That August, she donated $100,000 to the Red Cross in Cedar Rapids, Iowa, to help flood victims. In November 2009, Swift performed in Britain as part of the Children in Need concert, donating more than $20,000 of her own money. She donated $500,000 to flood relief in Nashville in May 2010 after the area was hit with deadly storms. In May 2011, Swift raised $750,000 from her Speak Now . . . Help Now! dress rehearsal concert to benefit Alabama tornado victims—a concert that would earn Swift an honor from the Do Something Awards. That July, she gave $250,000 to benefit the Alabama organization Nick's Kids, also for storm relief.

To Swift's and her fans' disappointment, several tour dates over the summer of 2011 were postponed after Swift came down with bronchitis and was advised by her physician not to perform.

> "There is a tendency to block out negative things, because they really hurt. But if I stop feeling pain, then I'm afraid I'll stop feeling immense excitement and epic celebration and happiness. I can't stop feeling those things, so I feel everything. And that keeps me who I am."[10]
>
> —TAYLOR SWIFT, QUOTED IN USA TODAY, OCTOBER 2010

But she came back healthy and planned to do more touring in 2012.

LIFE AS A GROWN-UP

Away from the road, Swift found herself spending so much time acting and recording in Los Angeles that in the spring of 2011, she bought a traditional three-bedroom home in Beverly Hills, California. She also bought a million-dollar home for her parents in Nashville. She could easily afford the real estate. In 2011, Swift rose to Number 7 on the *Forbes* celebrity power chart, with earnings topping $45 million.

Even with growing fame and fortune, Swift told *USA Today* she still took time for the little things that made her happy, such as walking through the hilly parks of Nashville, talking to friends, and baking. When she wasn't performing or writing songs, she watched a lot of television, especially crime shows. Her interest in history had her visiting museums when she was on tour and reading books about John Adams, Abraham Lincoln, and Ellis Island.

||||||||||||||||||||||||||||||||||||||||||||||||||||||

ENCHANTED FUTURE

In July 2011, Swift announced she would be joining the ranks of celebrities with their own fragrances. She named the perfume Wonderstruck, based on the lyrics "I'm wonderstruck" from the song "Enchanted."[11] Produced by cosmetics company Elizabeth Arden, the fragrance became available in stores in October 2011.

Swift launched her own fragrance, Wonderstruck, in 2011.

As 2011 wrapped up, Swift wasn't done performing. She had big plans for 2012. In addition to more touring, she would be voicing the character Audrey in the 3-D animated film adaptation of Dr. Seuss's children's book *The Lorax*, which was slated for release in March. She hoped to do more acting in the future.

She was also writing songs for her next album. According to Swift, her writing switch was never turned off and she had been writing new songs since *Speak Now* was released. In a YouTube Q&A video, Swift explains she needs to write 40 to 50 songs to end up with the 13 or 14 she considers good enough to make into an album she's really proud of.

Swift is still writing songs about her personal life whenever and wherever she can—in airport bathrooms on paper towels, on her tour bus in the middle of the night, recording them into her cell phone. She may not discuss her relationships, but they're happening, though the Taylor Nation might have to wait until her next album is released to find out the details. When asked in a 2009 interview what kinds of songs she would be writing in the future, Swift answered, "I write songs about my life. When my life changes, so will my music. It's as simple as that. I tell stories."[12] Taylor Swift's fans surely look forward to whatever musical stories their favorite artist will have to tell.

||||||||||

With upcoming film projects, a new fragrance, and several albums under her belt, Swift's career seems to be just beginning.

TIMELINE

1989

Taylor Alison Swift is born in Reading, Pennsylvania, on December 13.

2003

Swift lands a development contract with RCA Records.

2004

Sony/ATV Tree Music Publishing hires Swift to a songwriting contract.

2006

Taylor Swift is released on October 24.

2007

On May 15, Swift performs "Tim McGraw" at the ACM Awards.

2007

Sounds of the Season: The Taylor Swift Holiday Collection is released on October 14.

2005	2006	2006

Scott Borchetta signs Swift to Big Machine Records.

On June 19, Swift's first single, "Tim McGraw," is released.

Swift begins touring as an opening act for Rascal Flatts on October 19.

2007	2008	2008

"Our Song" becomes Swift's first Number 1 single on December 22.

On July 15, the extended-play CD *Beautiful Eyes* is released.

Swift receives her high school diploma in July.

TIMELINE

2008

On November 11, Swift's second album, *Fearless*, is released.

2009

Swift's television-acting debut in an episode of *CSI: Crime Scene Investigation* airs on March 5.

2009

On April 23, Swift kicks off her Fearless Tour.

2010

Swift receives four Grammy Awards on January 31, including Album of the Year, for *Fearless*.

2010

Swift appears in the movie *Valentine's Day*.

2010

Swift's third album, *Speak Now*, is released on October 25.

2009

Kanye West interrupts Swift at the VMAs show on September 13.

2009

Swift is the most-played artist on the radio.

2009

Swift appears on *Saturday Night Live* on November 7, acting as both host and musical guest.

2011

On February 9, Swift's Speak Now World Tour begins.

2011

In May, Swift raises $750,000 to benefit Alabama tornado victims.

2011

Swift releases her Wonderstruck fragrance in October.

GET THE SCOOP

FULL NAME

Taylor Alison Swift

DATE OF BIRTH

December 13, 1989

PLACE OF BIRTH

Reading, Pennsylvania

ALBUMS

Taylor Swift (2006), *Sounds of the Season: The Taylor Swift Holiday Collection* (2007), *Beautiful Eyes* (2008), *Fearless* (2008), *Speak Now* (2010)

TOURS

Fearless Tour (2009–2010), Speak Now World Tour (2011)

SELECTED FILM AND TELEVISION APPEARANCES

Hannah Montana: The Movie (2008), *Jonas Brothers: The 3D Concert Experience* (2009), *CSI: Crime Scene Investigation* (2009), *Saturday Night Live* (2009), *Valentine's Day* (2010), *Dr. Seuss' The Lorax* (scheduled for 2012 release)

SELECTED AWARDS

- Won 2007 CMT award for Breakthrough Video of the Year
- Won 2009 MTV VMA for Best Female Video
- Won 2010 Grammys for Best Country Song, Best Female Country Vocal Performance, and Best Country Album and Album of the Year for *Fearless* (2009)
- Won 2011 ACM award for Entertainer of the Year
- Won 2011 CMA award for Entertainer of the Year

PHILANTHROPY

Swift has donated her time and millions of dollars to charitable organizations and efforts around the world. One of her first charitable acts was participating in a campaign to inform kids about the dangers of online predators. After witnessing firsthand the devastation caused by floods in her hometown of Nashville in 2010, she's given generously to areas of the country hit by natural disasters.

"I write songs about my life. When my life changes, so will my music. It's as simple as that. I tell stories."

—*TAYLOR SWIFT*

GLOSSARY

amplifier—An electronic device that, when combined with speakers, increases the sound of electronic musical instruments.

Billboard—A music chart system used by the music-recording industry to measure record popularity.

chart—A weekly listing of record sales.

crossover—A broadening of the appeal of an artist that is often the result of a change of the artist's medium or style.

debut—A first appearance.

demographic—A certain portion of the population, such as age group or gender.

extended play (EP)—A musical release with more than one song or track, but not enough for an album.

genre—A category of art, music, or literature characterized by a particular style, form, or content.

Grammy Award—One of several awards the National Academy of Recording Arts and Sciences presents each year to honor musical achievement.

headliner—The main act of a show.

karaoke—A device that plays the instrumental tracks for a selection of songs to which the user sings along.

lyrics—The words of a song.

mentor—A person with experience in a specific field, who guides someone with less experience.

pop—A commercial or popular style of music.

record label—A brand or a trademark related to the marketing of music videos and recordings.

signing—An artist agreement, by signing his or her name, to a contract (such as a recording contract).

studio—A room with electronic recording equipment where music is recorded.

tabloids—News organizations that focus on celebrities and celebrity gossip.

track—A portion of a recording containing a single song or a piece of music.

venue—A place where events of a specific type are held.

ADDITIONAL RESOURCES

SELECTED BIBLIOGRAPHY

Caramanica, Jon. "My Music, MySpace, My Life." *New York Times*. The New York Times Company, 7 Nov. 2008. Web. 12 Sept. 2011.

Frere-Jones, Sasha. "Prodigy: The Rise of Taylor Swift." *The New Yorker*. Condé Nast, 10 Nov. 2008. Web. 12 Sept. 2011.

Grigoriadis, Vanessa. "The Very Pink, Very Perfect Line of Taylor Swift." *Rolling Stone* 1073. 5 Mar 2009. Print.

Kotb, Hoda. "On Tour with Taylor Swift." *Dateline*. MSNBC.com, 31 May 2009. Web. 24 Sept. 2011.

Willman, Chris. "Taylor Swift's Road to Fame." *EW.com*. Entertainment Weekly, 5 Feb. 2008. Web. 22 Sept. 2011.

FURTHER READINGS

Cartlidge, Cherese. *Taylor Swift*. Farmington Hills, MI: Lucent Books, 2011. Print.

Spencer, Liv. *Taylor Swift: Every Day Is a Fairytale: The Unofficial Story*. Toronto: ECW Press, 2010. Print.

Vaughan, Andrew. *Taylor Swift*. New York: Sterling, 2011. Print.

WEB SITES

To learn more about Taylor Swift, visit ABDO Publishing Company online at **www.abdopublishing.com**. Web sites about Taylor Swift are featured on our Book Links page. These links are routinely monitored and updated to provide the most current information available.

PLACES TO VISIT

Country Music Hall of Fame and Museum
222 Fifth Avenue South
Nashville, TN 37203
615-416-2001
http://countrymusichalloffame.org
The museum highlights the history of country music and its stars with exhibits, videos, performances, and special programs.

The Grammy Museum
800 W. Olympic Blvd., Suite A245
Los Angeles, CA 90015
213-765-6800
http://www.grammymuseum.org
Located in downtown Los Angeles, the museum includes exhibits, interactive experiences, films, and special events related to all forms of music, the recording process, and the history of the Grammy Awards.

Nashville and Music Row
Nashville Convention & Visitors Bureau
One Nashville Place
150 Fourth Avenue North, Suite G-250
Nashville, TN 37219
800-657-6910
http://www.visitmusiccity.com
Visit the Grand Ole Opry and take a walk through Music Row, where Taylor Swift got her start.

SOURCE NOTES

CHAPTER 1. HER DIARY BROUGHT TO LIFE

1. Melanie Dunea. *My Country: 50 Musicians on God, America & the Songs They Love*. New York: Rodale, 2010. Print. 72.

2. Taylor Swift. "You Belong with Me: Lyrics." *taylorswift.com*. Big Machine. n.d. Web. 8 Oct. 2011.

3. Swift, Taylor. "The Outside." *taylorswift.com*. Big Machine. n.d. Web. 27 Sept. 2011.

4. Jon Caramanica. "My Music, MySpace, My Life." *New York Times*. The New York Times Company, 7 Nov 2008. 12 Sept. 2011.

5. Benji Wilson. "Taylor Swift—the Meteoric Rise of Pop's Brightest New Star." *Daily Mail*. Associated Newspapers Ltd, 25 Oct. 2009. Web. 9 Sept. 2011.

6. Swift, Taylor. "My Story." *taylorswift.com*. Big Machine. n.d. Web. 15 Sept. 2011.

7. Chris Willman. "Taylor Swift Confronts Mayer, Laments Lautner in New Album." *Yahoo Music Blogs*. Yahoo! Inc., 18 Oct. 2010. Web. 15 Sept. 2011.

CHAPTER 2. GROWING UP TAYLOR

1. George Hatza. "Taylor Swift: Growing into Superstardom." *readingeagle.com*. Reading Eagle Press, 8 Dec. 2008. Web. 15 Nov. 2011.

2. Benji Wilson. "Taylor Swift—the Meteoric Rise of Pop's Brightest New Star." *Daily Mail*. Associated Newspapers Ltd, 25 Oct. 2009. Web. 9 Sept. 2011.

3. Katie Cook. "CMT Insider Interview: Taylor Swift (Part 1 of 2)." *CMT News*. MTV Networks, 26 Nov. 2008. Web. 15 Sept. 2011.

4. Ibid.

CHAPTER 3. TAKING ON NASHVILLE

1. Vanessa Grigoriadis. "Taylor Swift in Her Own Words: The World's New Pop Superstar on Boys and Breaking into the Bigtime." *Rolling Stone*. Rolling Stone, 20 Feb. 2009. Web. 13 Sept. 2011.

2. Jon Caramanica. "My Music, MySpace, My Life." *New York Times*. The New York Times Company, 7 Nov. 2008. Web. 12 Sept. 2011.

3. Benji Wilson. "Taylor Swift—the Meteoric Rise of Pop's Brightest New Star." *Daily Mail*. Associated Newspapers Ltd, 25 Oct. 2009. Web. 9 Sept. 2011.

4. Jon Caramanica. "My Music, MySpace, My Life." *New York Times*. The New York Times Company, 7 Nov 2008. Web. 12 Sept. 2011.

5. Hoda Kotb. "On Tour with Taylor Swift." *Newsmakers on Dateline*. MSNBC.com, 31 May 2009. Web. 24 Sept. 2011.

6. Tom Roland. "Taylor Swift: The Billboard Cover Story." *Billboard.com*. Rovi Corporation, 15 Oct. 2010. Web. 3 Oct 2011.

7. Joe Edwards. "Taylor Swift Scores Hit Single as Country Music's Youngest Star." *Daily Herald*. Daily Herald, 26 Nov. 2006. Web. 28 Oct. 2011.

8. Taylor Swift. "Our Song: Story." *taylorswift.com*. Big Machine. n.d. Web. 15 Sept. 2011.

CHAPTER 4. OPENING ACT: ON THE ROAD

1. "Taylor Swift CMT Insider." *dailymotion.com*. wowow1, 15 Feb. 2007. Dailymotion. Web. 20 Sept. 2011.

2. Bobbi Smith. "Rascal Flatts Concert Review—Air Canada Center—November 1, 2006." *About.com County Music*. About.com. n.d. Web. 20 Sept. 2011.

3. "On the Road with Kellie Pickler and Taylor Swift." *GAC*. Scripps Networks, LLC, 26 July 2007. Web. 20 Sept. 2011.

4. J. Freedom Du Lac. "Taylor Swift Puts the Kid in Country." *The Washington Post*. The Washington Post, 28 Feb. 2008. Web. 20 Sept. 2011.

CHAPTER 5. *FEARLESS*

1. Taylor Swift. "Fearless: Story." *taylorswift.com*. Big Machine. n.d. Web. 15 Sept. 2011.

2. Chris Richards. "Taylor Swift, 'Fearless' and Full of Charm." *The Washington Post*. The Washington Post, 11 Nov. 2008. Web. 21 Sept. 2011.

CHAPTER 6. HEADLINER AT LAST

1. Hoda Kotb. "On Tour with Taylor Swift." *Newsmakers on Dateline*. MSNBC.com, 31 May 2009. Web. 24 Sept. 2011.

2. Hoda Kotb. "On Tour with Taylor Swift." *Newsmakers on Dateline*. MSNBC.com, 31 May 2009. Web. 24 Sept. 2011.

3. Daniel Kreps. "Kanye West Storms the VMAs Stage During Taylor Swift's Speech." *Rolling Stone*. Rolling Stone, 13 Sept 2009. Web. 9 Sept. 2011.

4. "Kanye West Interrupts Taylor Swift's Speech at 2009 MTV VMAs." *YouTube*. YouTube, 14 Sept. 2009 .Web. 27 Sept. 2011.

5. "Obama Caught on Tape Calling Kanye 'Jackass.'" *TMZ*. TMZ, 15 Sept. 2009. 28 Sept. 2011.

CHAPTER 7. LOVE AND MUSIC

1. "Taylor Swift Monologue." *Saturday Night Live*. Hulu, n.d. Web. 28 Sept. 2011.

2. Ibid.

3. Taylor Swift. "Speak Now: Story." *taylorswift.com*. Big Machine. n.d. Web. 15 Sept. 2011.

CHAPTER 8. FOREVER AND ALWAYS

1. Rob Sheffield. "Taylor Swift: Speak Now." *Rolling Stone*. Rolling Stone, 26 Oct. 2010. Web. 20 Sept. 2011.

2. Jon Caramanica. "Taylor Swift is Angry, Darn It." *The New York Times*. The New York Times Company, 20 Oct. 2010. Web. 27 Sept. 2011.

3. Rob Sheffield. "Taylor Swift: Speak Now." *Rolling Stone*. Rolling Stone. 26 Oct. 2010. Web. 20 Sept. 2011.

4. Swift, Taylor. "My Story." *taylorswift.com*. Big Machine. n.d. Web. 15 Sept. 2011.

5. Rob Sheffield. "Taylor Swift: Speak Now." *Rolling Stone*. Rolling Stone. 26 Oct. 2010. Web. 20 Sept. 2011.

6. "Taylor Swift." *Rolling Stone* 1137: 28. 18 Aug. 2011. *Ebsco Academic Search Elite*. Web. 14 Sept. 2011.

7. "Taylor Swift: Lyrics on Arm Are Like a Mood Ring." *Cambio*. Cambio. 8 Aug. 2011. Web. 31 Oct. 2011.

8. Jon Parales. "Her Fans, Squealing, Won't Hold Their Peace." *New York Times*. The New York Times Company, 21 July 2011. Web. 3 Oct. 2011.

9. J. Freedom Du Lac. "Taylor Swift Puts the Kid in Country." *The Washington Post*. The Washington Post, 28 Feb. 2008. Web. 20 Sept. 2011.

10. Brian Mansfield. "Taylor Swift Learns to 'Speak Now,' Reveal Her Maturity." *USA Today*. Gannett Co. Inc., 23 Oct. 2010. Web. 9 Sept. 2011.

11. "Taylor Swift to Launch First Fragrance, Wonderstruck." *UsWeekly*. Wenner Media. 15 Jul. 2011. Web. 3 Oct. 2011.

12. George Hatza. "Taylor Swift: Growing into Superstardom." *Reading Eagle*. Reading Eagle Company. 8 Dec. 2008. Web. 12 Sept. 2011.

INDEX

ABOUT THE AUTHOR

Melissa Higgins is the author of many nonfiction books for children and young adults, with topics ranging from appreciating diversity to biographies of people in the news. She also writes short stories and novels. Before pursuing a writing career, Ms. Higgins worked as a mental health counselor in schools and private practice.

PHOTO CREDITS